Pursuit
From Darkness to Light

Darian V. Pleasant

Editor: Ian Jones

Photography: Janet Mendez

DEDICATION

To those on a journey.
To those who recognize they were destined for much
more.
To those realizing that a life with Christ is a life worth
living.

SPECIAL THANKS TO:

Kevin & Crystal Pleasant

Marybeth McElroy & Family

Kevin & Cindy Lewis

Drake Burns

MY STORY

Graduating from Oklahoma State University was a very big milestone in my life. Often times it seemed like becoming a college graduate would never quite happen. Not to mention, it took me several years with a few breaks in between. Although I was very aware I was on my own journey, and no two stories are quite the same, it was tough seeing so many of my peers moving on with life.

After graduating, I thought the next steps were the same for everyone. Apply for a job, get the job, and begin your career. Life has never been that straightforward for me. Where most see a straight path, mine is typically full of twists, turns, ups, and downs. So, I began applying for jobs all around Oklahoma. Very few of those jobs spoke to my passions. I went on several interviews and got very few job offers. I also began to realize things were not necessarily working in my favor.

It was shortly after that I became very depressed. Nothing seemed to be working for me. My plans had fallen through, and in my best attempts to move forward, I could not see my next steps. Hope, for the time being, seemed lost. This resulted in me not going to church, and spending the majority of my time alone. I left my apartment for work, food, and on the weekends to meet my friends at the local bars to hopefully forget what I was facing internally.

I was lost. I did not recognize myself. I often questioned who I was, and where I was. For a two-month time period, I was tormented. I was afraid to be awake because I felt so alone. I was afraid to lay down at night due to the ugly thoughts that plagued me, the nightmares, and the very real presence of fear. I was often taunted by thoughts telling me how worthless I was, how far I had fallen, and what is the point of being here if I have no purpose. These thoughts harassed me every night by trying to convince me to take my life.

Thankfully, I never came close to taking my life. Even in the midst of darkness, God was still speaking. I remember laying in bed one day with tears in my eyes, and darkness surrounding me on all sides; I said to God, "Will you rescue me? Please, rescue me!" With a few weeks left before leaving Oklahoma to head back home, the fog slowly began to lift. Moving back home to New Jersey was never in my original plan, but I knew in my heart it was necessary for my restoration. In order to gain a fresh perspective home is where I needed to be. I made the decision to pursue that freedom no matter the cost.

Even after my move I still had this empty feeling inside. It was something I couldn't shake and constantly made me feel uneasy. It was one night on my drive home from work I told God, "I am not getting out of this car until this feeling is gone and something changes." I began to cry out to God, and war for my life in prayer for what seemed like two or three hours. When I stepped out of the vehicle I knew and sensed that something was different. I was free.

From that moment on, I began to dream again. Life was bright and full of color. I declared that I would never go back to that place of darkness. God told me to write, and that is what I began to do.

Whether you view this book as a journal, a devotional, a book of poems, or memoirs, I hope that it blesses you. They were written during my intimate moments with Jesus. They best illustrate and convey this transformation that occurred in my life.

This is for those of you who may have walked through a similar experience. May you be reminded of how faithful our heavenly Father is. This is for those of you who may be in the beginning stages of this transformation yourself, may you be encouraged, Jesus loves you and is walking with you. If you are someone who is in a dark place, this is for you. Remember that you are loved. Nothing can separate you from the love of God (Romans 8:38-39). Even though things seem pitch black, God is still calling you, speaking, and is fighting for you.

If you are struggling with suicidal thoughts, I want to encourage you to speak up. Find someone you trust. Don't keep these thoughts to yourself. The lie is that you are alone. The truth is that there is a God that loves you, and is willing to fight on your behalf. He is present and waiting for you to simply ask Him to come into your heart, and rescue you.

"The people who walk in darkness will see a light. For those who live in a land of deep darkness, a light will shine" (Isaiah 9:2, NLT).

*If you find yourself urgently needing to speak with someone you can call the suicide prevention lifeline below. *

National Suicide Prevention Lifeline - 1-800-273-8255

CHAPTER 1

LOST

Hello. Can you help me?

Do you know where I belong?

I misplaced who I am,

Or maybe I never knew.

I've been fumbling and stumbling to get back home.

There's blood on my shoes.

Even with three heel clicks, I'm still lost.

Can you help me?

Once a geyser erupting with love and compassion.

A tsunami washed away my joy.

My grip loosened.

The ground shifted and left a crater in my heart.

Who am I?

Depression haunts me.

Fear torments me.

Sadness grips my heart, and lies grip my mind.

I am worthless, maybe I shouldn't be here.

What place do I have? What change have I caused?

Who have I inspired? What have I ignited?

I hate myself.

I can't make a right decision.

Drawn to chaos and division,

I've said no when it should have been yes.

I've gone left when love was in the other direction.

Where are you?

CHAPTER 2

FOUND

01.04.18

Here I am.

Face to face with this freedom that often feels so elusive. But here it is.

Completely free.

What seemed so far months ago is now within arms reach.

Rescued.

As the enemy flees I run towards light. Catch me Lion of Judah.

Finally weightless.

Let freedom ring. Let freedom ring. Remind me how wanted I am.
Show me my value, because for so long I have felt so unloved.

Priceless.

01.06.18

Oh, how you love me. You see, that's what won me.

It's like encountering that first love and you're soon swept off your feet. You have captivated my heart with your essence, your presence, your grace, your mercy.

I am consumed by your unfailing love. I am wrecked day in and day out by tsunamis of your spirit.

You see, I am a mess, but you love me anyway. You have transformed me. Now, like Jeremiah I feel this fire in my bones, and like David I just can't sit here; I have to get up and move.

Oh, to be in tune with you. Like hearing a beautiful song that brings chills to your whole body.

You are that fresh breeze you never want to leave. That warmth of sun on your face you never want to escape.

You still call me your child, when my behavior and actions have not said, "Abba Father."

You love me. You love me. It's true, you love me.

01.08.18

You found me.

Even though I thought I was well hidden.

You found me.

Buried amongst pain. Covered by anger.

You found me.

You told me I was good enough.

You told me that you bought me.

You told me what you thought of me.

CHAPTER 3

TRANSFORM

01.10.18

What is this sound? This burning in my stomach. This pulling on my heart.

I still get scared at times. Yet, I feel you moving.

I am at the edge of this thing, and I am ready to jump. I am ready to live, truly live.

With freedom beneath my wings I am ready to soar.

Release me, and with fearless stamped across my heart, I will run and won't look back.

If you set my feet to dancing, victory will be my song, and I will dance with not a care in the world.

01.13.18

This has been the longest journey. I have always chosen the road less traveled.

With every tough decision, every labored breath, every sleepless night,

You were there with open arms, love filled eyes, and grace-filled hands.

How beautiful you are.

I have run on my own, but it doesn't compare to running by your side.

CHAPTER 4

LOVE LIKE NO OTHER

01.13.18

Wrap me in your arms. Your love is so disarming.

Fused with peace. You simply turn in my direction and every storm becomes still.

Tears fill my eyes. One breath from you and I am face to face with freedom.

As you began to speak, every false expectation, every label, and every lie instantly falls. Truth quickly rushes in; I am lifted.

Swept off my feet, running on clouds. Who is this? That can jump start my heart without uttering a word.

If the scenario were changed hundreds, of thousands, of millions of times, you would choose me again and again without hesitation. Telling me, "I am worth it."

You are madly in love with me. There is no story of blessing or turmoil that I can tell without sharing of your love, grace, and mercy.

You are amazing.

01.18.18

What love is this that can calm the seas?

That brings peace to the storm in my heart.

This love, that eases the raging rivers in my mind.

Wave after wave your presence covers me.

As I wade in your waters I am renewed.

I am made whole.

CHAPTER 5

FIRE STARTER

01.20.18

If you look for me now you will find me ready.

You raised me up. You poured out your heart for me.

And in those moments every fear vanished, every anxious thought dispersed.

Now, I finally see, you've been preparing me all along. You have equipped me for battle.

It was then when my faith was tired, and the road ahead became harder to see.

With every step through treacherous terrain,

You were there. You were there all along.

01.20.18

Can you hear it?

Freedom ringing in the atmosphere?

Can you feel it?

As it shakes you to your core. That fire in your fingertips. That jump in your legs. That dance in your feet.

Embrace it.

Can you see it? Chain after chain.

Shame dissipates, fear fades.

Loving fire consume me. Transform my heart.

01.20.18

You are the fire starter.

You ignite and set ablaze.

You fuel me.

Wreck me completely, day and night, until I am pliable and moldable.

You give me peace in the chaos.

Your strength surges when I am weak. You give the courage to speak. The boldness to leap. Your love detached every fear.

You are faithful to catch.

You are constant.

CHAPTER 6

CLOSE

01.22.18

How sweet it is to be close to you.

To dwell in your presence. To commune with you.

Letting go of the day, and abandon all at your feet.

Fill me up until I am overflowing. Expand my borders. Enlarge my heart.

Infuse me with your presence.

This is where healing takes place. This is where I am made whole. Restore me.

Fill me up until I am abounding.

01.23.18

Will you come? The door is wide open.

Will you run through it?

I have adjusted your ears to hear me better. You are limitless with me.

Will you run? I have cleared the path for you. Take what is yours.

You are not forgotten.

Adjust your stance.

I haven't ignored you, look at how I've altered your surroundings.

Will you only stay where it is comfortable? Or will you grab hold of this courage I have birthed in you.

Run.

01.23.18

You cause me to jump for joy. You birthed a song of freedom in my heart.

I am letting go.

Untie the knots. Break these chains. Tear down my walls.

For years I have built barriers around my heart.

In moments, as I rest in your presence, they are undone.

As you hold me I feel complete.

Your waves crash over me, my mind is renewed.

I am letting go.

01.26.18

Jesus, you sing over me.

You play a sweet melody on my heart strings.

You are strumming a new love song within me.

My feet dance to your tune. I sway to to the rhythms of your beauty.

You fill me with wonder. You are a beautiful mystery.

Continually in awe of the way your love washes over me.

The way your love rinses fear, and removes worry.

01.26.18

Daily I hunger for more of you. Daily you are faithful to fill me.

Your presence is pleasing to me. I am overjoyed with the thought of sitting before you.

As I inhale your fragrance I am instantly reminded of your goodness, how sweet you are, and how you have captivated my heart.

No matter how far I have wandered, you stood with arms wide open, excited for me to find my way to the open seat at your table.

I don't ever want to miss a moment with you.

01.29.18

To be in your presence.

To stand before you.

To sit at your feet.

Here is where I lose it all. I just want to be with you.

Take me deeper.

The intensity of your presence overwhelms me.

I want more.

I am not satisfied with just a little. Fill me up.

01.29.18

Throughout the day you surge around me.

Your arms are wrapped around my heart.

It's like I've been jolted by electricity; every part of me tingles.

It is your peace that runs through. It's your presence.

My night turns into day. Darkness fades. Heartache leaves.

Once again, I am met with your love.

CHAPTER 7

TALES OF VICTORY

02.05.18

Your love isn't elusive. Your blessings are abundant.

In you I find all that I need.

You have given me the courage to step, and the boldness to run, even when the path ahead has yet to be revealed.

You found me, and I have never been so free.

02.08.18

In the midst of chaos and despair, it's never chaos to you.

You have already seen me in this moment.

I can hear whispers of my success and songs of my victory.

You have made a way.

During desolate times, heartache, and pain. Buried in darkness, in a sea of depression, hit with swells of fear, you came to my rescue.

You heard me calling, and you showed up.

Like a superhero, you saved me.

In moments, depression was gone.

Fear vanished.

You mended the broken places, and you called me home.

I am yours.

02.09.18

Day after day your spirit calls to me, and my heart responds,
"Lord, here I am."

Your faithfulness engulfs me.

Take me deeper.

I will continue to draw near to you.

Misery turned to hope.

Once adrift, now home is where you are.

02.09.18

I will continue to press as you pull. I won't resist as you stretch.

As seasons change I'll follow your lead.

Shift me. I trust you.

You've arranged my steps.

Extract what limits my connection and my intimacy with you. Take me higher.

Transfer me out of comfort, show me something unique.

I desire something different.

Adjust my eyes. Chorus my ears.

Sync my heart beat to yours.

02.13.18

You raised me back to life by singing a new song over me.

Beautiful melodies infused with love, forgiveness, and peace, changed the cadence of my heartbeat.

You restored my joy and compassion.

You are the king of kings full of grace unending, love unconditional, and joy abounding.

You are the rescuer, healer, and protector.

Oh, how you love me. Oh, how I need you.

May my life scream of your glory and wonder. You hold me in your right hand.

You've given everything to prove your love.

May my life roar of your grace and forgiveness.

02.15.18

I awake to rays of your love peaking through my window.

My heart responds to your spirit with open arms. You are near.

Wherever you are you can find me there, in your shadow.

Constantly within embrace's reach. I can't afford to miss a step.

In you is everything I need.

02.20.18

Let it resound. My redeemer lives.

You have set me free.

You reach in, and you pull out.

You consummate my faith.

What can I face that you have not triumphed? What can I experience that you will not walk me through?

I'm drenched in love. Enveloped in peace.

You whisper, "Be patient."

I will not fear the future. I will not fear things not seen. Jesus, you are my sure thing.

02.21.18

Your presence is here. You are all around.

This is where I find my healing. This is where hope is restored.

Search my heart.

You are mending the cracks with unconditional love. You dress me in robes of peace. Cover me in blankets of truth.

Here, I can rest in your arms. Here, I find your strength.

On bended knees, with a heart poured out, here is where I draw closer to you. Where I run to you.

I don't have to be afraid.

I am picking up the pace.

02.22.18

I don't have to be afraid.

This love is unlike anything I have ever known.

With ordered steps, regardless of the circumstance, I find myself where I am supposed to be. Jesus you are good.

This love fills me up. It wraps its mighty arms around me.

This love kills lies and prepares the way for truth.

You'll never have to be afraid again. Walk boldly without fear. Run without looking back.

This love has made a way for me.

CHAPTER 8

I NEED YOU

02.23.18

I need you. I can't spend a moment without you,

My faithful king. My present help.

Like a child to its mother, I will follow you.

Great are you Lord.

As time with you increases, I only recognize how essential you are to my existence.

I never want to be satisfied.

Fill me. Then fill me some more.

I need you.

02.27.18

You are the burden lifter.

You brush away worry. You obliterate fear.

I need to be close to you. In connection with you is where freedom reigns.

I am filled with joy. Your peace brings tranquility.

Here I find my grit, where I become steadfast.

Your grace is sufficient, and my weakness is overlaid in strength that can not be matched.

You are the lover of my soul, and I am your beloved.

03.04.18

Your faithfulness is free of charge.

Your joy is a treasure.

You vibe within me. I feel you.

You've shifted my mind from anxiousness and worry to peace.

Search my heart. Make it more like yours.

I eagerly wait for my daily embrace with you.

Time spent with you transforms me to my core.

I need you. Minute by minute, hour by hour, let our heartbeats become one.

Every movement, every word, every thought, teach me this dance of love and peace.

I run to you and you lift me. I jump and you carry me.

Uproot and pull me deeper.

CHAPTER 9

DESTINY

03.31.18

I will stay in this place. In constant communion with you.

As I pursue you, I never forget who I am.

Reveal the ins and outs of the way you love me.

You speak to the longings and the yearnings of my heart.

Abide in me. I will rest in you.

You hold my destiny in your hands.

29373777R00031

Made in the USA
Middletown, DE
27 December 2018